# MYSTERIOUS DETECTIVES: PSYCHICS

By
Tamara Wilcox

A

Book

From

RAINTREE CHILDRENS BOOKS
Milwaukee • Toronto • Melbourne • London

Library of Congress Number: 77-14315

Art and Photo Credits

**Cover Illustration by Lynn Sweat.**
Photos on pages 8 and 16, The Granger Collection, New York.
Illustrations on pages 10, 27, 29, 33, 35, and 44, Sam Viviano.
Photos on pages 13, 19, 20, 24, 31, and 36, Wide World Photos, Inc.
Photo on page 14, Culver Pictures, Inc.
Photo on page 40, A. Pelschonek, courtesy of Beverly Jaeger.
Photo on page 45, Paul Ockrassa, St. Louis Globe-Democrat.
All photo research for this book was provided by Sherry Olan.
Every effort has been made to trace the ownership of all copyrighted material in this book and to obtain permission for its use.

Library of Congress Cataloging in Publication Data

Wilcox, Tamara, 1941-
  Mysterious detectives: psychics.
  SUMMARY: Discusses how some of the world's psychics have helped to solve crimes.
  1. Parapsychology and criminal investigation—Juvenile literature.
[1. Parapsychology. 2. Criminal investigation] I. Title.
BF1045.C7W54   133.8   77-14315
ISBN 0-8172-1061-X lib. bdg.

Manufactured in the United States of America.
ISBN 0-8172-1061-X

# Contents

Chapter 1
"Hurkos Has a Hunch"
Peter Hurkos                                    5

Chapter 2
"Tracer of Lost Persons"
Gerard Croiset                                 24

Chapter 3
"The Chicago Sleuth"
Irene Hughes                                   30

Chapter 4
"The U.S. Psi Squad"
Beverly Jaegers                                39

# Hurkos Has a Hunch
# PETER HURKOS

It was an evening in autumn. The streets of the city were crowded with people going home from work. William Van Derk, a young coal miner, had turned the corner and was making his way up the clean, quiet street to his small house. He was almost at the front step when two shots rang out. William Van Derk fell across the narrow step, killed instantly.

At first the Amsterdam police were puzzled by the murder. Within two weeks they had put together enough clues to suspect Van Derk's stepfather. But they could not find the gun he had used. Without it, they felt they had no clear case against the stepfather. Detectives had searched every square inch of the stepfather's home, the streets he would have used after the murder, and his car, *but the murder weapon could not be found.* The chief of police made a desperate move. "Call in Hurkos," he ordered.

The young man, Peter Hurkos, studied the case for days. He questioned the detectives at length and examined all the available photographs and evidence. He concentrated most on objects that belonged to the murder suspect. Within a week he gave his answer. "Look on the roof of the murdered man's house," he said. The police were puzzled. The crime had not even taken place in the victim's house. Certainly the police had been over every inch of the suspect's house. Now they were to search the murdered man's roof. But they decided to follow Hurkos' advice. They had nothing to lose.

When the police searched the roof, they found a gun lying in the rain gutter. The gun had been fired twice. What's more, the stepfather's fingerprints were on the handle. The police finally had the evidence they needed to convict the murderer.

Who was this Peter Hurkos? How could this young man—a former house painter—have known where the gun was hidden? He didn't even know the murdered coal miner or his stepfather.

Peter Hurkos is a *psychic detective*. He carries no gun, he wears a raincoat only when it rains, and he doesn't "slug it out" with the crooks he is after. But Peter Hurkos is thought to be one of the best detectives in the world. He is one of a small group of psychics whom the police departments of every country call in when their own detectives are completely baffled about some crime.

Psychics are believed to have some sense beyond the ordinary five senses most of us have. This sixth, or extra, sense is thought to be so well developed in psychics that they get important hunches (strong feelings) about things they couldn't have known in any ordinary way. No one yet has been able to explain what the psychics' sixth sense is all about, but scientists are trying to find out. The name they have given the extra sense is ESP (*extrasensory perception*).

This book will describe some of the world's outstanding psychic detectives. These men and

Sherlock Holmes—the famous storybook detective—would have been replaced with a psychic detective, but his creator, Sir Arthur Conan Doyle, received so many protests from Holmes' fans that he gave up trying to kill off Sherlock.

women are the beginnings of a new kind of police force who will make life harder and harder for criminals around the world.

Peter Hurkos was born in Holland. At an early age, he began to work with his father, a house painter. He seemed, in every way, an average, hard-working young man.

One day, in 1943, Peter Hurkos was helping his father paint a local school. To work on the ceiling, Peter had to climb to the top of a high ladder. His foot slipped near the top and he fell 36 feet to the floor.

Hurkos lay unconscious in the hospital for three days. When he finally recovered, he found himself with a fractured skull—and an astonishing skill he never knew he had. Hurkos seemed able to read the thoughts of another patient, a man he had never even seen before. He knew this man had sold a gold watch his father had left to him. He knew the man had been feeling guilty about selling his father's watch. But how could Hurkos—a stranger—know that?

Hurkos also advised a surprised nurse not to lose her friend's purse on a train. The nurse couldn't believe what she was hearing. How could her patient have guessed about the purse, when she had only just lost it and had not dared tell anyone about it? The nurse immediately had Peter Hurkos examined by a psychiatrist.

The doctor found nothing wrong with Hurkos. He found nothing unusual about his mind or thinking ability. *But Peter Hurkos*

How could Peter Hurkos have known that the embarrassed nurse had, just that day, lost her friend's purse?

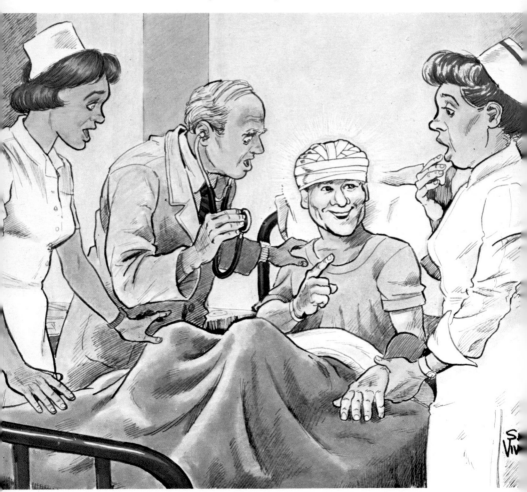

*would never be the same.* For the rest of his life, he would find that just being near people was enough to "cause all kinds of ideas to float through my mind."

When Hurkos left the hospital, World War II was raging, and his homeland, Holland, was occupied by the Nazis. Hurkos immediately joined the Dutch underground movement, a group of loyal Dutch men and women who secretly tried to make life hard for the Nazi enemies who now ruled their country. These "freedom fighters" put Peter Hurkos' gifts to good use. Hurkos was often able to tell people what had happened to their friends and relatives who had been captured by the Nazis.

Once, the leader of the Dutch underground showed Hurkos a photo of a Dutch freedom fighter. The leader asked Hurkos what his feelings were about the man in the picture. Hurkos told the leader that he felt this member of the Dutch underground should be wearing the uniform of Nazi Germany. Hurkos was sure the man was a traitor to the Dutch underground. It wasn't long before the leader had real proof that the suspect was, indeed, a traitor. By the end of the war, word of the "Hurkos Hunches" had traveled through the underground groups of countries throughout Europe.

After the war, Peter Hurkos was asked to work as a psychic detective for police departments in England, France, Germany, Holland, and the United States. He uses a method called *psychometry* to uncover information about crimes. Hurkos claims that by touching an object, he can "see" something about its owner.

Hurkos describes psychometry: "I touch. Then I see the pictures and hear the voice." Sometimes he needs to concentrate on the object for long periods of time. At times, he even sleeps with the object. At other times, Hurkos is able to give remarkable information immediately about a person sitting across from him in a room or shown to him in a photograph.

The hunches of a psychic detective are not accepted as evidence in a court trial. Each "message" the psychic crime fighter gets must be proved before it can be taken as evidence. For this reason, the police find it difficult to use psychic detectives. When they do use the help of detectives like Hurkos, the police don't always admit that they were given psychic help. Here is a Peter Hurkos case that is a perfect example.

Peter Hurkos claims to have psychic powers. He says he can "see" the unknown by combining his sense of touch with some mystical "extra" sense he has.

Hurkos' talents were not widely known in 1950, when word spread throughout the entire world of a major robbery. England's famous *Stone of Scone* had been stolen from Westminster Abbey. It happened right before the coronation of Queen Elizabeth II. For over 600 years, all the kings and queens of England were crowned in front of that stone. Word went

13

The Coronation Chair of Westminster Abbey in London is more than 675 years old. Almost every English ruler since the year 1300 has been crowned in this chair.

out to Scotland Yard—the London police force
—*find that stone right away.*

Even the famous detectives of Scotland Yard could not find the Stone of Scone. In desperation, they asked police in Holland to send Peter Hurkos to help. Though Hurkos knew these British police didn't fully believe in his abilities, he decided to help anyway.

He went to Westminster Abbey and knelt down before the coronation chair, placing his hands on it. He remained this way for 20 minutes. Then, for more than two hours, he concentrated on the crowbar that was used to break into the Abbey. Finally, he spoke. Hurkos told the detectives of Scotland Yard that the Stone of Scone was in a church in Glasgow, Scotland. He said he "saw" that some students had stolen it as a prank.

The police went to Glasgow where they discovered the Stone of Scone exactly where Peter Hurkos said it would be found. The case was solved and Hurkos' talents as a psychic detective would seem to have been proved. *But were they?*

"Scotland Yard," headquarters of the London police force from 1890 to 1967. This is an engraving from an 1890 London newspaper.

Something happened that Peter Hurkos says he never could have expected. Scotland Yard denied that Hurkos had helped them to recover the famous stone. In fact, they said, they had not even invited him to help. To this day, Hurkos insists that his side of the story is true. But Scotland Yard sticks to their version. However,

16

Hurkos says he was not discouraged. Though he is paid very little money for his services, he continues to help when his powers are needed. In an interview with a reporter from *Psychic Magazine*, Peter Hurkos tells of another fascinating case.

"Once when I was in Palm Springs [California], the chief of police called about his friend, a pilot, who was missing on a flight. I told him to bring some personal object from his friend's belongings, like clothing. The chief called the Air Force base outside of San Diego, and the base sent up clothing from one of the pilots.

"When I got the clothing, I asked for a map of the general area they were flying and began getting information about what happened. I sensed the plane was off course and I saw an explosion. I saw only two people in the plane and one out of it . . . all dead. Nine hours later, they saw the plane where I said they would. I was only a mile off in an area of 600 miles."

In 1964, Peter Hurkos was called by the Boston police. They wanted him to join the search for the "Boston Strangler," who killed several Boston women he had never even met

17

before. Hurkos was given many objects to hold to see if he could find any clues to these crimes and the name of the mad killer. Hurkos took pieces of clothing that had belonged to the victims and photos of the murder scenes. Hurkos astonished the police by telling them specific details about each of the stranglings. The police already had much of this information, but it had never been made public. Hurkos was able to describe the killer and was even able to locate the places where the victims had been found! Hurkos helped police artists to draw a sketch of the killer. This led to the arrest of Albert De Salvo—the "Boston Strangler."

At the beginning of the Patty Hearst kidnapping case in 1974, Hurkos was contacted by a member of the Hearst family. Hurkos was asked to come to San Francisco to help find Patty Hearst. Hurkos said that it would be too dangerous for him to come. He says he feared her kidnappers would become frightened and harm Patty. Instead, Hurkos had a member of her family bring a piece of her clothing to him. No one knows to this day what happened at that meeting between the Hearsts and Hurkos.

At the time of Patty Hearst's kidnapping, however, Hurkos had told a friend that the girl

Albert De Salvo—the "Boston Strangler"—was captured with the help of Peter Hurkos' "extra" sense. He helped sketch De Salvo—a man he had never seen.

was kidnapped by a group of rebels. Hurkos also said that Patty Hearst had been brainwashed by her captors. He said that there would be shooting and death before Patty Hearst would be found. His predictions were remarkable, considering that he "saw" and described all these

Under a cloud of mystery, unclear to this day, Peter Hurkos was involved in solving the Patty Hearst case.

events accurately many weeks before the true story became known.

In the interview in *Psychic Magazine*, Peter Hurkos was asked if he has to keep proving his abilities to the police. Hurkos replied: "Usually, yes. But not with the ones I worked with previously and who know me. And when I go into a new area, I always work *with* the police, never behind their backs."

Hurkos added that the police always doubt a psychic detective who works with them. He concluded: "I think that it is strange that most policemen will take tips from practically anyone, but when a psychic comes along, he has to prove that he can help."

What Peter Hurkos says about the police attitude toward psychics is often true. However, in one case at least, the Dutch government has actually given a *license* to a psychic detective. He had to pass difficult tests, but he is probably the only psychic legally recognized by his government. His passport reads: Occupation— Clairvoyant. His name is Marius Dykshoorn.

Like Peter Hurkos, Marius Dykshoorn was born in Holland. Unlike Hurkos, however, Dykshoorn didn't have an accident before he became aware of his psychic ability. From an early age, he always seemed to know things before they happened.

For more than 30 years, Dykshoorn has been a psychic, helping the police whenever he can. His cases have been very successful, but there were stories in many newspapers when he solved one particular case. It was solved entirely over the telephone. He had never met any of the people involved in the case.

Franz-Josef Becker, the captain of a river barge, telephoned Dykshoorn from West Germany. He said that his boat had been stolen and asked the psychic to help find it. After looking at a map of the area where the boat was last seen, he told the captain that the boat had not been stolen but set adrift. Dykshoorn also told the captain where his boat could be found.

Two days later, Dykshoorn got another telephone call from Captain Becker. Becker told him that the boat had been found exactly where the psychic detective had said it would be. However, the cabin had been broken into and a large amount of money was taken. The police had been told, but the captain wanted the help of Dykshoorn. Once again, by telephone, the detective told him to go to a nearby barge and find a boy who was about to leave on vacation. He told the captain that the money would be found in the boy's travel bag.

Captain Becker told the police and they went to the barge, found the boy, and recovered the money.

The Becker case was not the only one that Dykshoorn has solved over the telephone. A man who lived in Belgium asked the psychic for help when his valuable dog had disappeared. The detective told him that he could see the dog tied up in the yard of a building. He also told the dog owner that he believed it could be a bakery. At least, the smell of fresh baked bread would come from someplace nearby. The building, he said, was half pink, half white, as if it was being painted.

The dog owner later told Dykshoorn that his valuable animal had been found by a guard at a bakery which was white but was being painted pink.

It is a mystery in itself that Holland could have produced two of the world's greatest psychic detectives. But there is a third important Dutch psychic as well. Gerard Croiset has also solved many baffling cases.

# Tracer of Lost Persons
# GERARD CROISET

Gerard Croiset has worked with the police in a dozen countries throughout the world. He has solved many baffling cases—murders, robberies, suspicious fires, and missing persons.

Croiset's psychic powers have been studied by the University of Utrecht in the Netherlands. This is one of the few schools in the world that works closely with psychic detectives, studying their methods and learning more about their ESP. Professor Tenhaeff, who is the head of the Department of Psychic Studies, has personally studied Gerard Croiset's abilities. When Croiset is called to assist the police, Professor Tenhaeff is usually present to study and document what happens.

One interesting case started when the parents of a missing boy telephoned Croiset directly. Their local police had looked for the child for two days but were unable to find him. After hearing details of the case, Croiset told the parents not to worry. He said that the boy was alive and well. He had simply taken his bicycle and gone off searching for adventure. Croiset says he "felt" that the missing boy had planned to go to the seashore in Belgium and then to sail away on a ship. Croiset said, however, that the missing boy might be home within two days.

When the impatient parents called the next day, Croiset told them he had been wrong. The boy had arrived in Belgium but would return to them the following Tuesday. On Tuesday morning, the parents again called Croiset. He told the worried couple that they would have news of their child later that day. Sure enough, the police telephoned the parents an hour later to say that they had found the boy bicycling along the Belgium coast. He was following the exact route Croiset had described to the police.

The mayor of a town in Holland witnessed another of Gerard Croiset's most famous cases. A young woman of the town had been robbed and beaten on the head with a hammer. The brave young woman managed to grab the hammer away from the man who had hit her. The criminal fled, leaving the hammer as the only clue. The hammer was shown to anyone who might know its owner. It was even displayed in a local shop window. But no one recognized the hammer or, at least, said they did.

The mayor called Croiset in on the case. The psychic detective felt able to describe the criminal. He said that the man was tall, about 35 years old, and had a deformed left ear. Croiset says he "saw" that the man wore a ring with a blue

Gerard Croiset claims to use his psychic power to "see" a criminal he doesn't know and describe him to a police artist.

stone. He also said that the hammer did not belong to the criminal but had been borrowed from someone else. Croiset went on to also describe the owner of the hammer and where he lived.

Croiset's detailed picture of the criminal reminded the police of someone they had questioned earlier on the case. Unfortunately, this still didn't give them enough evidence to charge the man with the crime. But a few months later, this man was arrested for another crime. After his trial for this other crime, the man confessed that he also had hit the young woman with a hammer. Everything Croiset had described to the police about the suspect proved to be true—except one. The police could never prove that the man owned a ring with a blue stone!

In an interview with Gerard Croiset that was filmed in Holland, a writer decided to test Croiset's ability to locate a missing person. The writer, however, tried to *trick* Croiset. The trick was that the "missing" person was actually a British naval officer who died in 1847. The officer's ship had been lost in Arctic waters while searching for the fabled Northwest Passage between the Atlantic and Pacific Oceans. Croiset was given a letter the officer had written to his sister in 1845, shortly before he left England for his ill-fated attempt to find the passage.

The letter was delivered to the psychic in a sealed envelope. Croiset was able to tell many amazing things about the "missing person," not by reading the letter, but by simply holding it. He said that the missing man was a "sailor, an officer, living in another century." Croiset's only error was that he said that the officer had drowned, when the man had actually died of natural causes after going ashore.

In the United States, two psychic detectives have become well known. One of them has predicted that someday an entire force of psychic detectives will be created to fight criminals. See if you agree.

Gerard Croiset could "see" a sailor who lived more than 100 years ago simply by holding a letter the man had written in 1845.

# 3

# The Chicago Sleuth
# IRENE HUGHES

Irene Hughes, a psychic who lives in Illinois, has been working with the Chicago area police for over ten years. Mrs. Hughes was born in a log cabin in Tennessee and comes from Scottish-Indian heritage. She claims she has had the gift of psychic power since her early childhood. This "gift" was inherited from her psychic Cherokee grandmother.

Hughes is a very well known psychic counselor and astrologer in the Midwest. She became

nationally known when she predicted a fire that
destroyed an Apollo spacecraft, killing the three
astronauts aboard. She predicted this disaster

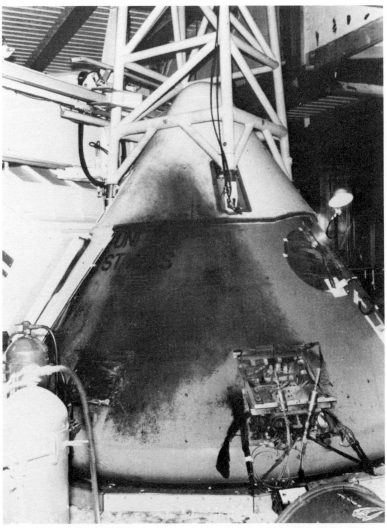

As Irene Hughes predicted, a fire ripped through this Apollo I
spacecraft taking the lives of three astronauts in a practice
countdown.

31

three days before it happened. When she tried to stop the fatal ground test of the spacecraft, her prediction was not taken seriously.

Her success as a psychic detective is remarkable even though Hughes can't explain her mental talents. Irene Hughes is one of the few psychics who has had a lasting and effective relationship with the police authorities. In a recent interview, Hughes was asked about her work with the police. She replied:

"I have worked on many cases. Once a police captain called me into the office and asked me to work on a murder case. The sergeant brought in a box and took out a human skull. He put it into my hands and said, in a gruff voice, 'What do you get from that?' I answered, 'A heart attack!'

"And then I told him the name of the person who had been murdered, and it was the police captain's turn to almost have a heart attack! I indicated the name of the place where I felt the murders had been contemplated. The police did find a place by that name and found that it was where the murderer had contemplated the first of five murders."

Irene Hughes says her psychic power told her the name
of the murder victim and the exact place where
the murder was planned.

Assistant Chief of Police, Virgil Jordan, of
the Kankakee, Illinois Police Department, be-
lieves in Irene Hughes. "I'm thoroughly con-

vinced that she has a deep perception, something that comes to her from a supernatural source." Chief Jordan has requested her services several times, including the time when she was able to help his department identify the killer of a policeman.

Two policemen visited Hughes with 20 photos of suspects and placed them on her table. Among the photos they brought were several of criminals in prison who could not possibly have committed the murder. The policemen asked Hughes to hold each photo. She proceeded to tell them about the subjects one at a time. She told the police the crime each person had committed and sometimes the criminal's name. The police wrote down all of Hughes' answers. Later, when they checked her answers against the police records of the people whose pictures they had brought, they were amazed at her accuracy.

Irene Hughes also told the police that a picture of the person they were looking for was not on the table. The police brought different photos for her. This time Hughes said that the picture of the man who had committed the crime was there. The photo to which she pointed was of a

Hughes accurately described criminals she did not know, and went on to identify the killer of a policeman.

suspect already in custody. Some time later this man confessed and was convicted of the crime.

A case that Irene Hughes helped solve in March, 1970, proved to be the most famous in

Irene Hughes, psychic detective, has worked with the Chicago area police on dozens of baffling cases over the last decade.

her career. On a bitterly cold night, the Chicago police were searching a South Side canal for the body of a man who had died in a shooting accident. They couldn't find the body, so they called Irene Hughes in on the case. *She solved the case over the telephone.* She asked the detective where they had been looking and he replied, "Over on the left side of the canal."

"No wonder you didn't find him," said Irene Hughes. "The body's on the right, way over there under some rocks. It is coatless and one shoe is missing. He is wearing a white shirt. He'll be found before Sunday."

The next morning, a young man walking along the canal found the body dressed exactly as she had described it. It was partly hidden by some rocks, but it was found before the police had searched in the area Hughes had indicated.

Mrs. Hughes has devoted her life to developing her special psychic abilities and using this talent for worthy causes. Recently, in a magazine interview, she described her wish. "I feel that there will eventually be a crime laboratory composed of psychics, and there will be a whole psychic force in the future working with the police. I really feel that the police are going to be far more open to this than they have been."

Her "feeling" may well have been a prediction of the work being done by another psychic detective—*Beverly Jaegers.*

# 4

# The U.S. Psi Squad
# BEVERLY JAEGERS

In St. Louis, a psychic detective named Beverly Jaegers has set up a "Psychic Rescue Squad." This may be the first of many such groups that will develop around the world. The St. Louis group consists of 15 trained psychics who use their powers to solve crimes and locate missing persons. Local police openly admit that they work with Mrs. Jaegers. She has an amazing knack for coming up with clues long after the police have exhausted every lead.

Members of Beverly Jaeger's "Psychic Rescue Squad," now becoming known as the "U.S. Psi Squad," hold regular non-police jobs. They meet each week for training sessions and

Beverly Jaegers, with members of her Psi Squad, opens a package of bullets taken from a murder victim in Mississippi.

to work on special cases. Jaegers compares the routine of the Psi Squad to athletes in training. She says members must exercise their "psychic muscles" to keep in shape.

Each member of the U.S. Psi Squad has his or her own special way of solving a crime. Some members of the group "tune in" to the location of the crime. Others "feel" a connection with the victims, while others can "pick up" the motives of the criminals. Beverly Jaegers and her group also have skill in handwriting analysis. They can often obtain important information from samples of the criminal's handwriting. Each group member adds his or her information to the picture. All these clues are finally fitted together like a huge jigsaw puzzle. Jaegers then goes to the police with the information.

The U.S. Psi Squad started as a study group. It grew into a crime-fighting unit in 1971. At that time, members decided to help find a missing person. The case, reported in the headlines of the St. Louis newspapers, became known as the *Lucas Case*.

Sally Lucas, a St. Louis housewife, had disappeared from a shopping center not far from where she lived. The police could find no reason for the disappearance and no clues as to her whereabouts. A close family friend gave Beverly Jaegers some of Mrs. Lucas' personal belongings. From these articles, the psychic detective says she received some strong feelings about the case. She described her thoughts to a crime reporter on the St. Louis *Globe-Democrat.* Jaegers' statements about the Sally Lucas case were so accurate that the reporter thought that Jaegers must have read a confidential police file.

When he later learned that Jaegers had never even seen the police files, the reporter paid close attention to some feelings she had about the case that were *brand new.* Beverly Jaegers said that she had a vision of Mrs. Lucas' car near a large body of water, maybe an ocean. The very next day, Florida police reported finding the car less than 50 feet from the Gulf of Mexico. A man was arrested and charged with kidnapping Sally Lucas, but there was still no trace of her.

The *Globe-Democrat* reporter called a friend of his on the police force. He told the police official about Beverly Jaegers. The reporter felt that the psychic might be able to help the police locate the missing woman. At first the reporter's police friend merely laughed, but he finally gave in. He decided to let Jaegers sit in Sally Lucas' car and see what kind of impressions she would get.

Jaegers sat in the missing woman's car holding tightly on to the steering wheel. She later described seeing "motion pictures flickering through my mind's eye." Her feelings were written down and later proved to be quite accurate. She described a murder and how it was committed. The victim, she said, was Sally Lucas. Her description of the murderer fit the man who had been arrested in Florida. She also saw a bridge (the body was later found near one), horses (the bridge was on a street called *Horse Creek Road*) and the letter "C" (Horse *Creek* Road was close to two highways—one called Highway *C*, and the other called Highway *CC*).

As she "saw" the crime acted out in her mind, Jaegers says the physical pain became so strong that she had to leave the car. She and her husband followed the map in her mind to a state park about 40 miles outside St. Louis. For the next two days it rained. The Jaegers and the police found the hunt for Mrs. Lucas' body difficult

Jaegers sat in the victim's car and "saw" the murder take place.

in the downpour. When the weather cleared, the police continued searching and found the body of Sally Lucas only a few feet away from where Beverly Jaegers had said it would be.

Jaegers' pinpoint accuracy in the Lucas case encouraged the U.S. Psi Squad to forge ahead. Members of the squad are now working with the police on several cases involving murders and

The body was found in the overgrown area, close to where Jaegers said it would be.

missing persons in the St. Louis area. Mrs. Jaegers has made the squad a licensed detective bureau so that the evidence it gathers can be accepted in the courts.

The U.S. Psi Squad only accepts cases referred to it by the police. In this way the psychic detectives always work with the cooperation of the local police.

Beverly Jaegers hopes to prove to all police departments that her kind of detective work is useful. Eventually she would like to be able to train police to develop their own psychic abilities. The growing number of psychics helping the police may be a sign that this is possible. Following are just a few examples of psychics who are becoming more accepted in the area of crime-solving:

- When Patty Hearst was kidnapped, former astronaut Ed Mitchell gathered together a large group of psychics to help locate the missing heiress.

- In Maine, psychic Shirley Harrison has been named Honorary Sheriff because of her work in locating missing persons.

- In Atlanta, Georgia, famed psychic Harold Sherman has assisted the police all over the country in solving crimes, just by discussing them over the telephone.

- In Arizona, psychic Mervin Hockenberry has helped the police locate downed airplanes for the Arizona Civil Air Patrol.

- In Sweden, psychic Olof Jonsson solved a mass murder case in which the killer was actually one of the policemen assigned to the case.

- The New York City police used psychics to help artists sketch a mass murderer they called the ".44 Caliber Killer," after the type of gun he used. The killer called himself "Son of Sam" in his teasing notes to the authorities. He killed six and wounded seven people in a year of night-time attacks. A "Son of Sam" suspect was arrested in August, 1977. The police sketch was used to help capture him.

Many police departments still deny that they use psychics. They often refuse to admit that their own crime-solving techniques do not, by themselves, always get results. Psychics, however, often work with the police behind the scenes. Individual detectives who would never admit it often consult psychics on their own. More and more police officials are turning to psychics when their own crime-solving methods reach a dead end.

It may not be long before an international psychic police force is established to take advantage of the special talents of the world's psychic detective.